INTIMACY

THE COLORADO PRIZE FOR POETRY

INTIMACY

Catherine Imbriglio

POEMS

Center for Literary Publishing
Colorado State University

For information about permission to reproduce
selections from this book, write to
Permissions, Center for Literary Publishing,
9105 Campus Delivery, Department of English,
Colorado State University,
Fort Collins, Colorado 80523-9105.

Printed in the United States of America.

Library of Congress Cataloging-in-Publication Data

Imbriglio, Catherine.
  [Poems. Selections]
  Intimacy : Poems / Catherine Imbriglio.
      pages cm. -- (The Colorado Prize for Poetry)
  Includes bibliographical references and index.
  2013 Colorado Prize for Poetry.
  ISBN 978-1-885635-33-4 (p : alk. paper) -- ISBN 978-1-885635-34-1 (electronic)
  I. Title.

PS3609.M37A6 2013
811'.6--dc23

2013035740

for Reginald Shepherd

Imagine hitting moonlight and living to tell.
—Michael Gizzi

Ha, ha's the final consequence.
—Herman Melville

CONTENTS

INTIMACY

RUSH INTIMACY

I.

I have no one to talk with about my behavior.

Light falls on the wrought iron chair on the chair on the weight of the chair.

As a matter of unpraiseworthy conduct, too much or not enough talking may be accompanied by periods of light insensitivity.

To measure out-of-body insensitivities, a girl should use quantitative instruments, such as calendars, rulers, clocks, string.

Many obsessive internal subjects will closely align with externally extreme behaviors, empire, stereo birds, in an aftermath of haste acceptance.

Let me direct you by a sidereal motion, as with hand or head.

She stands, bare breasts to the window, as if to encounter her invasive tendencies.

Simultaneously, public and private spaces form and blend.

Though in simply not telling, you might receive a solid rush, so you'll do it again, as with burglar recidivism.

I omit the porch omit the man on the porch.

She lives in a place where talking on a cell phone while driving is the ritual equivalent of spiritual depth.

As when viewing the body of the washed mother, you should pay attention to your visual processing.

I move that her house is a box with a vertical column.

I move that the house is three boxes, the house is a technical term.

The sign says room and spirits.

To talk to an available city hall representative, press zero.

What is the first word the first word is rescue rescue is the first word.

2.

I get jolted awake by traffic sounds, squealing brakes of a truck moving too quickly down the hill.

If a rush to start is not the same as a rush to complete, maybe you can court sleep by not saying anything.

Though I can no longer make excuses for you, which includes no longer making excuses for myself
        making prior excuses.

It limits my character, like tripping over a wire, light speeding through.

The agéd mother laughs ho ho ho.

I expect the light, expect the light to be about the light.

When a married woman says to an unmarried woman, my sons, it reflects a hierarchy.

A girl takes note of superior words: carotid triangle, frontal sulcus, nasal spine.

The pith can be used for producing a wick, which produces a halo effect.

Or would you be simply acting normally, as in a flash mob, crowd adjustment by crowd adjustment.

Other contrite functions do not illuminate disgraced temporality in an impulsive nation, haste makes waste, fever dew, slob ice, bastard acacia.

Shocking objects on the porch wouldn't know that person.

The painter moves into a crawl space under the house, wager against an actual passing.

Hurry in the form of plaited dissonance runs away with her, photo of a naked man on a leash, local hijinks—name something hollow that tarnishes.

On the sidewalk, members of the flash mob, following email instructions, ring bells and blow whistles for forty seconds, emulating leadership fantasies.

Yet another speedy index is a change in electrical conduction response, gold rush pending gold rush, Junelight pending Junelight.

A grown-up might tell her to sleep on it.

LARGHETTO INTIMACY

I.

Though she has not been formally diagnosed, she suspects she may exhibit traits associated with a childhood anxiety disorder known as selective mutism.

In social settings, she can talk easily one on one but has difficulty when three or more are in the room.

Signs of selective mutism include a consistent failure to speak in gatherings where there is a generally agreed upon expectation for speaking.

Afflicted children often present in their first year of schooling while continuing to speak normally at home.

In one traced population, 58 percent refused to speak to the teacher and 20 percent spoke to no one at school.

SM is usually distinguished from extreme shyness though both are likely to be comorbid with other socialization difficulties.

Girls play with dolls, they don't swaddle favorite red metal shovels and take them to bed.

One might attribute SM behaviors to an oppositional nature, though some clinicians have found anxious and oppositional behaviors in the same child.

Phrases such as "let's not get carried away" or "that isn't happening" shouldn't be endlessly practiced for just the right vocal entrance.

Rumor has it one student used his fist to break a classroom window a few days after an ill-informed teacher tried to force him to read aloud.

Often in conversation with acquaintances, she stumbles over names and ordinary small talk like "Hi, Harry, how's it going?"

Is her continued fascination with repetitive musical behaviors opportunistic or a purposeful engagement with
the inhumanity of the linguistic code.

A father and a mother may be ill-advised if they think their daughter will grow out of it.

You shouldn't bring a book to a party or family gathering and spend hours reading by yourself as a safety mechanism.

Daisy, Daisy, give me your answer, do.

A common denominator may be a neurodevelopmental immaturity that makes afflicted children react badly to
sensory overload.

For example, how do you say "what a mess" in a teasing tone.

For a Carthusian monk, the absence of spoken language impresses on him the singularity of each moment.

Five will get you ten he will not tell you of his god cart, glowing.

Even days later, you could still see the knuckle cuts on the young man's hands.

2.

Though she was often mute, she found herself preoccupied with internal word bursts.

Spider glass, spider glass, spider in the glass, alas, alas.

At night she really did hear her clock ticking ten times more loudly than ordinary, an auditory hallucination
not unlike Poe's.

Unlike children with other conduct disorders, often mute children are not seen as a bother.

This one conjures up a giantess for acting out hairyscary disagreements with nearby "higher-ups."

There has been little research about the course of the disorder into adulthood, so the eventual removal of symptoms may not necessarily be indicative of a successful turnabout.

Whose boundaries are confused.

However, one could argue that it is the very fact a person does not speak that makes her more noticeable.

Impressed upon her is anything that rests on a silence, so as to install weighty moments, lengthening ear reach, wool after the carcass has decomposed.

The worst carnage came north of Baghdad at a Shiite funeral.

Implosive findings suggest a familial resemblance between speech avoidance and nonaccountable spectatorship.

She could sit with the father for hours in what she thought was a comfortable silence.

Silence! Silenzio!

Still, she thinks she might manipulate her environment by being silent, a refusal not unlike Job's.

Or that silence can help you with forming neural intimacies, unlike coming to your subjects already predisposed.

Brain be nimble, brain be quick.

The president says his decisions were based solely on conditions on the ground.

She reverts to about-face maneuverings, forms for speaking when there are no expectations for speaking, broken ear nests, deathbeds on paper, an aluminum skull.

Lotus seeds 1,200 years old have been sprouted in China.

For the monk, death may be simply "my death," an alter ego, a winnowing.

THING INTIMACY

I.

She places two ladybug magnets on her refrigerator.

The ladybugs are red with black spots, good luck belongings handed down to her, circuitously.

Imagine animating your things so they could simply fly over, while you remain stationary.

Underneath, none of them are solid, just like you, replete with rabid energies in motion, subatomic bed-rocking.

Listen up when deploying above-board coarse-grained mimicries.

You'll mainly notice a thing if it breaks or goes away, viz., in selling the house, we had to discard many things our elders had accumulated.

Doorstops, bookends live on past them as depreciating testimonials, along with the trees and shrubs they planted.

Yet you are not supposed to want for too many things, a desire for things not considered a higher order of wanting.

Still, she remembers a story about a boy who was bored with his everyday things, so they all went away.

Except for one sympathetic blanket, he had to sit on the ground naked and shivering.

Fancy the set of communal axioms aimed at that boy's thing hatred.

My things cry out to be dusted or at least touched: cookbooks, rocking chair, copper-plated teapot anticipating heirloom ontology.

She asks me if I want to live with her: what about my things?

There are latent obligations hanging over you, not just things.

The afghan's red squares, held together by white borders, organizes homegrown flight paths by way of the deceased crocheter's fingers.

There were many more of those charming magnets, but my brother threw them away.

Quick, touch that thing!

There are things she needs to do today, laundry first, among them.

Bring me that blue thing from that closet; put it over there with those other things to be taken away.

Was that a sex cry or a cat cry, from the neighbors?

Here's the thing.

Suppose that _____.

Suppose that she supposes a spirit residing in the ladybug magnets on the surface of the refrigerator doing a spirited ladybug thing.

You have been invited to speak on behalf of what things?

In the living room closet she keeps two purloined x-rays of her skull, from which to develop a thinged intimacy with her head's interior: brain, eyesockets, sinuses.

The boy's things did come back when he said he was sorry, extending a here-there liminality, like each key on her piano.

Expect dizzying side effects—humiliation, shame—when she takes on the filmed head's subject-object ambiguity.

As when after the earthquake, you need transport vehicles to get things to the damaged island, not disappearing solaces.

Like the repentant boy, she apologizes to her things, acknowledging in them excess metaphysical presence, cultural fantasy: fetish, value, totem.

Probable causes, happenstance bind music box interiority into her solid state appurtenances, "I beg your pardon" motivating aura, wish in the real or fake coccinellid, skill in joining.

2.

Lately, I've been "caught up in things."

He was fighting his decline, but does not remember he put 39 photo albums together for his children.

Here's a photograph of an evicted woman on a sidewalk with all her household things.

Think of eye-catching, literally, your eye being tossed around by your things.

On her piano is a gold statue of an elongated woman playing a violin.

The heavy-metaled woman would make a good defensive weapon, if someone broke in.

Likewise, stolid gadgets holding down the virtual realm stir up residual grace, soul, atemporal utopia.

Over what's inside the thing, her nominal adulty-hood superimposes digital war games, plants zapping zombies with seed missiles.

Appalling visitors to the substructure seek out vital innards with more than just idle curiosity, child picking apart a beetle.

She used to picture soul as a leaky pail, sometimes a thimble.

If so, what to do with continuous grace drippings.

Wistful gradients on the emission, absorption spectrum require formal generosity in assessing another one's cherished objects, frog collection, glugging fish pitcher.

Time to set limits for sorting out statistical illusions underlying the constant clutter.

How about if she pleases herself with a clown face instead?

Draw it on her nose, brows, cheeks, lips, forehead, implementing virtuous space, history of her object-sense, then open wide, molecular letters in ragged greens, blues, yellows!

The nursing home staff calls the WWII veteran's assisted bathroom visits "toileting."

Seek forgone intimacies with him in recollection of tadpoles, oak galls, jack-in-the-pulpit sightings, even those all too frequent arguments over insect repellent.

The young army lieutenant brought home a miniature English-French dictionary dated August 1944, a gift from Georges Illy, who may have been a French soldier.

M. Illy wrote his name on all the odd-numbered pages of his 624-page book, which fits inside her closed fist neatly.

If beauty is pleasure regarded as the quality of the thing, don't be surprised if underneath the thing there's probably an überclown that says, don't get comfortable.

Hence, the dictionary is becoming all that's left of times past between unknowable soldiers.

Est-ce que c'était si tôt? et qu'est-ce que vous avez fait pendant ce temps?

She depends on inconspicuous blossoms from backyard tulip trees to ward off aesthetic casualty from over-ripe economic systems.

Good heavens if I have been bombarding you with bricolage, intimacy as contingent as yarn culture!

The blossoms resemble a yellow-green cup, with yellow pistils and stamens, orange splashes at the base of the sepals, perfect flowers for decorative bowl floating.

She wishes that in the bowl she could float him three thousand years of memory blossoms, Etruscan jewelry, Da Vinci diagrams, Mezzogiorno.

Can she exchange her bowl's forms of value for her clowned forms of value, visible or invisible?

Believe me, I am not dodging the question of the trivial.

Though evoking tender scenes or touching objects by cultivating memory wishes might make even a remotely emotive daughter crumble.

You can see why the ladybug magnets opt for their right to remain humble.

LAWS OF MOTION INTIMACY

for Rosmarie and Keith Waldrop

I.

I watched an inchworm cross the width of the deck, humping itself up, a body without ventral prolegs
plank-measuring.

The momentum of the worm is frame dependent, like my trafficking in sweet mouth.

Laws describing the momentum of forces acting on the worm's body and my body will elicit a sense of
where each body is going.

Similarly, a first word exerts a force on a second word, enticing a third.

Little errors will compound themselves.

Hip girdle, heave away ho.

So as in almost all wars, rational discourse tries to forestall glimpses of its nonsensical material base, Suzie
Rottencrotch, Short Arm Inspection, to prevent a search and destroy from inching through.

Pelvic ambushes can host rational discourse, but not the other way around, so you won't
be able to just sit there comfortably.

Does one say more from an avoidance point of scrutiny, such as rhubarb under my window: rue: barb.

Use "as if" as a mobile device, use all laws, use "as if" as if there were no other ethical ways of doing.

Rubber heels are a good choice for walking on dry macadam roads.

Clothing must not bind or rub.

The sense of acceleration or turning in the inner ear, even the motions of muscles and bones can be caught word-worming.

Rational discourse won't tell you if you are slapping an angel around.

2.

Splashing in a sea with three-foot wave heights might be a little like slapping the angel.

She's afraid the angel will slap back harder, but not on any consequential level would an angel be involved.

Water proof, wind proof, what other proof?

A fit walker's pelvis sways easily, when she is striding along.

Sand underfoot demarcating a lighter to a darker brown rules in a law of aesthetic probability, giving her her value.

Use "as if" as a mobile device, use all laws, use "as if" as if there were no other ethical ways of moving.

Your feet may increase appreciably in size.

He might be going downhill or he might get better after an infusion of fluids.

Wayfarer, your affair moves slowly.

Embed fourteen aesthetic thrashings you would not have otherwise, never mind the angel.

He is not where his body is, buccal cavity to her excessive thin-lipping.

As if _____.

If movement follows movement (Heraclitus), will a good mouth-off follow along.

Rational discourse will not tell you how much you are lamed by not "as-if"-ing.

3.

The pelvic mechanical system transfers weight from the trunk to the lower limbs, for walking or standing, as if
holding itself responsible.

In a nonrational discourse, you can have inside voices, swing low sweet, that time of year thou mayst,
veteran nonsense.

I was jumbled, I was wrote, round and round we go, language flashing its biology.

Walk on, walk on, blameless from a molecular vantage point, as if you were a soldier.

The worm is a caterpillar that will become a geometric moth, plank-measuring only for a limited amount of time.

The rule is, when following orders, to whose advantage.

Use "as if" as a mobile device, use all laws, use "as if" as if there were no more ethical a way of ruing.

Use a pastel pencil to mark where the curious dog got the worm on the deck.

Explosions cause more casualties to the ranks: reuse booby traps, rocket propelled grenades, mortar and artillery
rounds as humped up points of comparison: intimacies in and out of our keeping.

Let the angel be a center of proleg gripping hooks, enticing leeway, empathy in adopting an attitude toward others, for example, enemy soldiers.

Let a river in summer look as if it were iced over, random sunlight posing you a thin freedom.

Severglass, severglass, sever in the glass, amass amass.

In such cases, carrying a larger knapsack for sprinkling nonsense, aesthetic activism over the terrain will not keep her in motion with the falling soldier.

To ramble on, cultivate balance, belated starlight, veteran motions-at-large, arms swinging rhythmically.

ON YOUR SIDE INTIMACY

I.

A relief to say I spoke to no one all day, rhyme not just sound but a visual trestle.

Objects, when they rhyme, secure your back, unlike the thud of the snow falling from branches, fallen clumps roughing up what was once smooth snow cover.

They aerate your soul, pull you to them.

If you had fastened on the storm, you would have seen how snow rhymes with shed rhymes with branch rhymes with window.

Comity with any landscape requires effort, so I began to think of the frozen cove in terms of argument rather than wave function.

Ducks don't freeze into the ice, they waddle on it.

The expressive ice does not coincide with the remembering ice though changing rates of tidal flow under the ice radiate my side of the cove with bumps and swirls, irregular freezing primed for the sake of composing this beautiful memory.

If an underlying scale of intensity allows for matchmaking across dimensions, what I call rhyme you might call resemblances.

As for the birds even ice is territorial, as when two gulls square off and then wing-beat, beak-wrestle one another.

Since when does rigidity not come up, associating argumentative habits with rictal patterns stunned into ice when the temperature prohibits replacement melting.

The consummate landscape responds with reversal, heat, snowy banks scaled back like composition of the moon when making different shades visible.

The halo around the moon, like my argumentative habits, undershoots nakedness, mood, embarrassment, range of plausible values in appearing to rhyme snow with ice trestles.

The effects of repetition on increasing familiarity extend to compromise, weathered rhyme-likeness, bird expectations of blue or green temperament.

No longer on his back, he has hers if they snuggle.

You can bet on a compensating moon taking the side of a beloved's charisma.

The lovers complement the moon's sky-rounds of buttoning and unbuttoning.

To understand this or any argument you must first make an effort to believe in it.

Then what's behind the lovers or the moon is on your side as a statistical intimacy.

2.

In the middle of the blizzard, a clown beat its way towards me.

After the storm the clown inflicts normal dry-eyed moon with phases of proper and improper grieving.

If I had lived by the cove in 1630, would I have known of the moon-clown's reputation for making randomness seem intentional.

Speech sounds uttered with the breath and not the voice are called surds, but when applied to mathematics surd indicates an irrational number.

How do talkers find so much to say to one another.

I didn't acknowledge I *was* grieving, making isolation a form of nourishing quiet the way light mixes with wind on the surface of the unfrozen portion of the water and you don't want anyone to hear you speak of it.

One of the fighting gulls pinned the other fighting gull, until they both slid along the ice, lost hold and then separated.

How many clowns are there if there is a clown for every moon in all galaxies.

I dreamed little disk moons kept rising to the surface of my skin and when removed they kept springing up as metal dog tags, war medallions.

Grieving in the dream, I erected a tent over the expanding medals for these war people.

Wakefulness in expressing solidarity with other persons is a matter of backing up incongruity properly, yellow crocus, lamb breath to stars spotting for other stars, planets, galaxies, hidden universes.

Of course, one realm depends on too small a scale, the other too large to lay claims to a reliable sampling.

He lays his arm across her, unstatistically.

She follows a set of bird tracks in the snow.

One evening in spring, light and wind will play over the returning tide, push forth parallel waves of different tones and length, rolling in a water embroidery.

The birds foreground light and wind's rhyming of the lovers as they refrain from speaking, harmonizing silence, fluidity.

Birds, lovers roll side by side, on this side of the moon, this side of the galaxy, embracing numeracy.

Loose spirit across matching bird dimensions releases this surd tone of underlying surd intimacy.

DO NO HARM INTIMACY

I.

The hypoglossal nerve is the twelfth cranial nerve, leading to the tongue.

I have been as you have been, touching up surfaces, aftermaths of so many nerves grizzling.

Like befitting a belief to a behavior, it could hardly be otherwise, belly holding itself to a standard, conflict, point of conflict, world beside us, battering ram, fawn.

My hand and your cheek exert electromagnetic forces on one another, if I brush against you.

A small touch spreads compassion, contact, what feels like contact, air holding itself against a bird.

Not the bird per se, but the angle of the bird, great blue skimming over the water: legato, legato, another legato.

As with the bird there are braking mechanisms for touching down on others' semi-legible surfaces, for example, on a father's acting or being acted upon.

Likewise for characters in a period film giving advice to one another, when there's a war on.

Though the film's war was a hundred years ago, she connects to undercurrents in the characters' "I wish you would" admonishments.

Blame this, blame that.

I cannot not take back what I said no matter how much I might want to.

Other members of the viewing audience mock the idealism, sincerity in the hero, from last week's episode.

Do you take this lawfully embedded harm, from which, through all subsequent judgments your character will be formed.

I admit that coming from the hero's tongue, a solicitous injunction could generate some wishful thinking if he
    says things like "I was wrong."

He pulls film moon and earth moon together, befitting apprehension to the world inside us, neap tide, moon
    being pawned.

2.

The hero has returned home damaged from the war.

He can't be beside himself properly, step away from domains not accessible in truth-telling propositional logic,
    birds exploding other birds with their calls.

In watching the film, I have cognitive not emotional empathy.

Take two could mean "ought derived from is," clown lip.

How else might I be?

The film prepares us for the world without us, trees, clown brigade, sea charisma.

The swans don't care or feel for it.

Every effort to represent the hero as a war casualty obstructs daily unimagined war casualties.

What's the harm in performing sympathy or regret with members of the cast even though the screen is
    beyond bereavement.

About-faces, tender scenes, touching second chances are inextricably caught up with the hero's replacement belief,
    when they're bringing home the bodies.

May I have a word: advice demands acknowledgement.

Get the hell out of my sight.

In the cove, wading birds go gracestalking.

Implementing a noble cause requires embracing incongruity, gags in transcendental logic, molecular impulse as good as starlight defending starlight.

Not at the time, but in retrospect, a daughter might say of the father, though I often felt battered by him, a bird not the same as its flaws.

3.·

I tend not to think of space/time as the world beside us coming apart.

Knowing whether or not the hero will improve is equally subject to fanfiction, anosognosia.

Do illusions make decisions palatable outside a narratable world, waterspace as room to breathe decreasing probability of ignoble thoughts, clown taking advantage of a bird.

Only grief has the right to expect so much of you.

Like, what was I thinking.

A young girl says, I am as plain as the nose on my face, so I can see the tale right through you.

She can always offer up good but erroneous explanations for the clown inside her, gunlight soothing gunlight.

Even if she is me, composite harms come in many flavors, beginning with up, down, charm, strange, top, bottom, from subatomic particles.

How long a value is that.

In the cove, men are out in boats, netting crabs.

Was revealing a father's bullying tendencies as harmful as a clown taking advantage of a bird.

As in the film, directed composition doesn't seem to screen in anything, if what happens next is the only reason you read something.

Can my tongue toggle between the father and the boatmen fluently.

Unlike earlier thinkers, who had sought to improve their accuracy by getting rid of error, Laplace realized that you should try to get more error.

In the right brain, clowns, birds, seek out freedom, pleasure in the world beside us, leaving for the left, light patterns, full moon to the cove's proximation of the moon, synapses to error literacy.

4.

After staring into the light to observe the opposite shore, I close my eyes and see blue bars against orange lids, inner eye extracting only the ship's smokestacks.

When I look again, the bars turn pink and float over nearby objects.

Color, sound, emotion are central for pushing awareness through the tongues inside you, pulling to the surface beliefs you have held but never registered.

For weeks after the father gave away the hydrangeas she had given him, the daughter hardly spoke to him.

Intimacy with the cove gives her surface reparation for emotional deficits when rewatching the hero.

Maybe making waves or holding dear to the world is consistent with elusive genetic longings, same as gunlight serving gunlight.

I need some advice: father, when is it as harmful to save you as not save you.

Be careful of what you wish for, mending of the hero, fan ecstasy, facts of dementia.

Even so, may my pushing and pulling go beyond a surface's molecular structure to actually deeply touch you.

Of course the hero's emotions are represented as complex and numinous in the storyline.

I can see with my eyes his eyes look blue, but only because I must act as if I'm certain of my light receptors.

Unlike the script version in which the heroine throws the hero over, in my inside world I don't throw him as far as I can trust him.

Viewer identification with him is clown deep with wading birds, degrees of impetuosity, acceptance of frog or fish victims.

So that harmfulness has only one degree of separation from him or you acted out underneath generalized relativity of clown performances.

Plotting back-up beliefs, temporary knowledge, floating memory of the film can have touch-up value, making the father larger or smaller, plausible according to telescoping screen size as frame for birds watching him stall in flight, leaving you to moon as guesswork, self as distal.

CHÂTEAU NOIR INTIMACY

for Bradford Robinson

The trope of a tree, the trope of the land that looks out at the tree. The trope that could be sawed off into lumber, the trope with which to build a house on the land. Beyond or through the trope there is always the turning toward it, as even here when I pause to strip a real birch of its bark.

If the turn is silly bussed, then what to make of it. Does it assemble lip-smacking good will for the contested subject. A discarded curl from the torn off bark. Let me pause to name vehicles with formative, i.e., nursery clown, intentions. Would I want to turn the trope of your fingers into fingers. Would I want to turn the smiling dark into dark.

A form of a pill bug turning the big ships in and out of the harbor. A form of a rhinoceros turning to the wrong kind of mud model. A form of a form sending all forms into reversal. In their reversals, will all forms echo and mrof.

A son kills his father and nearly his mother. Turning or not turning what is your liability, come figure how it on the diagonal, come figure what's up down then across.

If I go out today, if I go out tomorrow, if I take with me a piece of chalk. Floppy, extra wide, dinner plate hibiscus. Called out, what by, and what for. Posture, change of posture, what you are amplifying. What's left when you subtract a real person from the chalked.

Man possibly bitten by bat, treated for rabies. Man arrested for a series of East Side robberies. Some changing of the guard in girls' ice hockey. Long drawn out application for sunshades appealed to zoning. Altering pensions puts city in uncharted territory. Some who lost family members become peace activists. Job worries escalate with recession costs.

Is it transgressive to try on the trope of another life, viz., what is its size, how does it fit, when do I wear it, do I feel foolish, yes and then some, in August the rose of sharon is out, the chicory is out, tell me again the laws of attention grabbing, why one thought comes and not another thought. If I turn to look at the tree, will the tree still be there, can I sit under it, or is it crossing over, if it is crossing over, what is confluence, what is a low contrast, what do you get if you cross a blue washcloth, a honey bee and a summer squash.

WHOM DO YOU TRUST INTIMACY

When everything you know is like a windlight shifting, is there ever a day to keep the sum of the wind as in the wave and the tree lights bending, to accumulate like the shapes you can never see directly, indirectly, to stow away like the effects of the invisible on the visible, to keep for yourself so much unintended motion, hey sailor,

between you and the wind is a recursive embedding, if storm predictions are less than accurate, if at the loading dock you see a green bag unattended, if you want to be something light, and a gust knocks you over, if retrieving a memory recasts the memory, a piling on for the tongue like the sum of a motor idling, a motor racing, hey there, you, from whoever *is* this that's speaking, if a bower springs from the beak of the bowerbird, do you put trust in its rigging, if the bird fails to secure a mate, is there a raftlike instability, as with the abled observing the disabled, as with the male bird's pitching and rolling, hey (yes) you, whoever is there amid the dock lines chafing, the channel markers dinging, why be a stranger, for if trust lies with hope, you can give a wave to the offspring, if one doubt forecloses another doubt, you can get Thomas on it, if every act of language distends the language, you can keep watch lest the tongue be claustrophobic, unless, come on there four bells, is this the wind having an episode, yes having an episode: as when a person stops being polite, that's the shift when you'll know him, if you are attacked while you're sleeping, ahoy the depths you'll be owned by it:

HINGE INTIMACY

for Reginald Shepherd (1963–2008)

1.

The hinge method of communication is a cultural tool for thinking upside down. TUD is an impure aesthetic, useful for backing up intimations of abnormality in the eyelid wars. Hinging in the dark it mimes the dark: how to pace your zounds. I do not hold to hinge transparency, though I respect anyone's need for believing in it. A hinge is a type of communication longed for, argued over, negotiated, according to the goods in bivalve shells. If you practice TUDs according to bivalves, you can swing from ancient rotation axes through which your every good has been hinged. Do not take hinge rotations lightly: Hinging is a reliable technology for reconciling qualitative self-management with quantitative therapeutic scores. Circle whatever applies: Foresight, hindsight, ox, head, eye, door. Once you calculate your results, you may wish certain hinge tendencies could be nixed, but everyone must take her hinge medicine: best with the sea shuttling beach stones over beach stones, with what they give as opposed to what a hinge gives off.

2.

Viz.: His decency is wider than mine, his indecency is wider than mine.

3.

Archaeological studies show that on the sides of Egyptian mountain passes the earliest traveler alphabets were hinged. Consequently, the contours of a hinged life should fill social closeness with the baggage of a travel surrogate. On my own walks, intimacy sometimes becomes a clown word for hinge. Clown goes summer assaulting into the night, got stilts, got nails, got rubber bands, clown goes seeping into the hingework, got corpse, got star height, got quite a huge repertoire of hinge. Stumbling down a steep trail to Mohegan beach, I found a walking stick on which my own clown limbs could fasten. So as on the beach each beach bend was serially hinged. That afternoon the bluffs were clay cat paws, gullied long and riveting. Every second a new clown jaw was being hinged. What holds you or it together, that rocky shore, the sea flipflashing? Dear metalepsis, love echolalia. To the traveler who pray-told the want from his experiences: (please find) a hinge through what you see there, from that what you were here to see.

FREE WILL INTIMACY

1.

She was chasing after "you" illusions like those black birds racing for the trees. A "you" can cast her attention on flight, a soaring after, or on atomization below the level of the spine, which Mei-mei I borrow from you, my thinking about spines, figural refusal or assent within some fated person in a garden, this one being teased into picking some of the foxgloves: go ahead, no one will notice, why not take a few of those white and purple bells. The Adirondack chair where she sits is on the river side of the garden, so her bird-watching can be a mealy-mouthed occupation, in which she blames incomplete information, out-of-sight out-of-mind slippages, bird visions fading the longer she fixates on them. If each neural hemisphere has a different sense of intention awareness, how *do* you distinguish mealy plum aphid, mealy starwort, colic root from within a grammatical person, neither here nor there in parceling out "you" treeing indeterminacy wisdoms. Seducing her will, seducing her won't. Meanwhile, underneath spines, gree eill trlsyiond trhulstly (free will relations regularly) cross explanation boundaries, covering over what you resemble it resembles, obscure use of devious language, free will incoherence opening and closing upon your choice no choice temptation windows. Just as amateur caregiving is an obligation well underway before a "you" is conscious of her will to do it, "No cause no cause" comes only long after Cordelia chooses. Me: I thank you much. She: Io limito. Io limito.

2.

Places you wouldn't go otherwise

Human in the nonhuman

3.

Later on, two fishermen on the river rocks, in line with the afternoon glare, so many light needles entering the eyes: water strobe light fishermen strobe light: what separates you from what you resemble, it resembles: jerky-eyed stop and go traffic—water filament flash flash body filament flash flash—"any chance you would" a cheap trick honking on your spinalhoods. Touch: touch touch touch: go. Within intimacy limits, there like accidental graphics calling out for better zone laws, sex work, sick person hygiene: I only meant, I would never mean to. And then the light path vanishes, settling vision water into every-day water, exploding silhouette into fisherman silhouette, needled eyes into common eyes, inclining without necessitating. Must you carry on. Ring ring hello.

Household feeding is largely responsible, an unpaid labor of planning, shopping, catering, in which the relation of human to individual is utter susceptibility to debts, moods, food acquisitions, brain nuisances. Conscious will *may* retain a right to veto action in the last milliseconds, for which there would be a neural preparation, local economy of favors, many saccadic pulsatings. The ability to do otherwise. Touch: touch touch touch go. Not all parties agree in this matter, you as a free will species with wayward letter TactiC8s, noticing hollyhocks, impatiens, lobelia, depending upon your olighthentsnglemsnts (light entanglements). You're not as sold. Thomas Hobbes, John Locke, David Hume, John Stuart Mill. In you: them. On purpose (tangle) in no purpose. Like light. When carrying on with its character(s). Whippoorwill. Whippoorwill. I/O whippoorwill.

TO THE LETTER INTIMACY

On the hill there is a low labyrinth, dirt pathway lined
with homely ground cover, weeds, grasses, vines.
She takes it as a tour puzzle, brain, leg, lung slow motions,
contemplative body in a set of immersed and immersing mediums,
spirit, ground, witness in walker, walker in witnessing.
What comes up is bubble structure,
offshore island in the form of a teardrop, water vapor, sea foam.
Shear and pressure forces, sound waves, shock waves
provide delicate bubble interactions between public and cell.
In the heat the green goes. Bubbles with a radius larger than 0.8 MM
spiral or zigzag as they rise. An off-panel character excites
a meander pattern in her thought balloons. Privacy is a discreet
value, an appeal to forgiveness, abolition,
as in air, speech bubbles, mood, order of intent,
"I don't hear you," a physical quandary in her brain shiverings.
She puts her fingers into her mouth.
Intimacy bears this moral charge,
short bursts of light emitted from imploding bubbles,
pressure inside and outside the sound wave, exacting as
an air entrainment, like the speed of sound through her clothes.

In the heat the green goes. What touches what in a non-directed graph.
Adult fantasy, Ariadne's thread through an alphabet topology,
the class of lowercase letters with one hole.
You wind your privacy in. You wind your privacy out.
Magnetic decency might mean polarization on the island.
The bubble in an old measuring level.   So.

The labyrinth overlooks Sachem Pond, North Light, Block Island Sound.
At the center walkers leave money, photos, hair clips, business cards,
impulse information in a ancient scribe line, rock, paper, instruction manual, ACTG,
genome, code. Friends, strangers not talking
is a visual intimacy, inside voices bubbling independently
of you, green darner zigzagging by her like a grace voltage.
Emotional division—let me go, don't let me go, compassion, rationality—humbles her
reverence limits for what goes on inside each person,
as each person's linguistic system is confined by a labyrinthine code.
She adjusts her quiet to her quiet, the way she might slide the light
gradually over the burnt grasses in the stored photograph, swatch of land
next to the labyrinth, thin air relations deepening outside
her hearing thicknesses. Follow the letters of the code.
A little way down the hill are roof triangles, three sections of house, powerlines.
The pond is like a bubble at the northern tip of the teardrop,
visual distance in a visual scarf, the silence beneath the sounds of her thinking, visible
and invisible in the motions of the dragonfly, as in its wind sewing.
At the center she seeks out air lines tied with air lines, mixed tones not present
in the original tones, a "to the letter" delicacy, name scratched on stone
with another stone, as if to underwrite the silence beneath her listening.

STREET INTIMACY

In 1917, the building opened as a majestic vaudeville house.
Its façade is white terra cotta, in the center a two-storied arched window,
gridded glass. Tacit street codes requiring vigilance for controlling emotional
display frequencies limit what she can see through to, white on green fleur-de-lis
patterns in the terra cotta, ten rectangular gridded windows
decorously balancing the orders of the facade.
Flat glass is now made by a floating process, molten glass spread over
beds of molten tin, to ensure smooth surfaces, uniform thicknesses.
The visual history of the fluctuating environment, in which the theater's ancestry
evolved, favors comic relief in having a thing for, as in stock performances
from Columbina, Arlecchino. She: you keep away from me. He: but yesterday, such
thigh. Twinned reflections in the building's windows further comedic short range orders,
long range disorders in the theater-going crowd, the way sand, soda ash, limestone,
dolomite might surprise her, randomizing potential heartthrobs
as within her glass consciousness, just as over any atomic distance you cannot predict
which intimate molecules in a glass will be proximately involved.

To learn street ecology, study light availability, hydrology, waste disposal,
savvy on-the-scene reflexes, street culture of instinctual judgments about race and crime.
He often tells her emotionally charged things only in the street, as a glass filter
that might seriocomically flatten her. Bouncing back to co-presence
sets off a molecular slapstick underneath her public feeling rules.
For sale bodies, for sale energy behaviors, time.
In its early days, the theater presented musical road shows or revues,
some bringing bare-breasted ladies or live elephants to the stage.
Her public flirtations with the theater windows vitrify then and now
relational inventories, renewable in the street, as if she were floating.
Renaissance wisdoms might bubble up in an adsorbing street scandal, moments
of commonality in the crowd, shoppers, tourists, vendors, sex workers, overnight
inhabitants spread to nonuniform thicknesses, binding danger, pleasure, humiliation
from the passing theater, until she is quick with the gravity of street fools.

LOOP THE LOOP INTIMACY

1.

I withhold these truths, in formula, from you, otherwise I am just leading you on, letting you think I know something you don't, that you are some place I'm not, that's why it is always so seductive, always to be locked into this connective, you with me with it, the exposed as is the case just now of how not to be rootbound, and you get a glimpse of it now in the yard, as water just over the trees, where you and I holding forth with such sentiment would, like the wind, be mathematical grounds for suspicion. As we

2.

The loops between air and water, pulling vast quantities of things I have been doing, it, but I withhold this also, sitting at the end of the rocks, slights she made so much more of them shopping, cooking, gardening because you have no basis for how I spend my that is of genuine or does he get a perverse kick out of letting her know you had better give up startling me out—here I wasn't a series of renunciations but doing it *pas seul* simply to *démarcher* you, in hopes that I can withhold this at the cottage with the dog and the rest all on the coast, when she got tired of that breakers that wash in from a single front you occupy to observe that is not yours and water, pulling vast quantities I wished for of heat and moisture into the atmosphere, into ripples and waves, into the changing patterns of water that tongue around the globe.

Air moving across water causes it to break

3.

Physics of law the same as to the causes of water across the break to it ripple into higher grown that. The way you see a stranger's mother similar undulations form in moving air. At the sea's surface he had two wave systems; they roll and push again each other. Unlike autism and literal ways of seeing, you blend as air and water, evading not only as individual elements. So as eventually the built sea

4.

If you push the way wind pushes water that hands me the flow to the right in the other hemisphere the speed of the wind that propels it, did you know the air moves faster than water, when I thought I'd take a crack at it the air it pushed water as if it were coolly mating its temperatures. Except for mammals and birds. But along coastlines temperatures may rise abruptly as different water masses bump and squeeze against each other. Except for mammals and birds, temperature, density, salinity might sound even more sexual.

5.
There is something about them

The waves

Of joy
Of linecut

6.
Can it be this
The way the wind pushes the water to the right in the northern hemisphere and to the left in the southern hemisphere so that it sweeps larval organisms away from predators.

7.
Things that were important on that account generally Adam I'll have to have Gloria assist you I so importunate, them the series sitting behind the series really when no one did, as up above deeply with the waves coming in, you make me feel so swimming. Be that as it never may, caress the roundabouts you occupy, rows for the them there they of at

from the cottage to seek right kinds of their they were bending them into, here a series of what knots, skinny-dipping. Between cooking my you had where you had my you them there synapses crossing over, loop renunciation loop the there they them looping the foxgloves looping the lobelia looping the then along comes back much of what you were syntactic method row row plant place row row plant place, the latter may be right in bracing the day, so receptive to outside pressures and influences.

TO THE READER INTIMACY

1.

I admit a discourse on value.

This goes to galaxy, moon, memory of any size: why on earth is the earth, why on backscattering thee backscattering.

Picture yourself as light spreading over river waters: thee setting a you off as clownwright.

Games, clowns, soul toys can freak out standard comfort measures, you stirring up blue, gray serial wavelets on behalf of number narratives.

Here a five knot wind coming from the south merges with solar winds to inflect what it is like to have one body now.

Infrared Andromeda's spiral arms will commensurate taste, lack of taste, if she multiplies herself by at least 70 billion of the known galaxies.

The left hand is the nonsacred hand for this childless woman gasping at progeny.

Three four five: once I caught a fish alive.

Watch out for antennae, beaks, sepals stepping up to protect your back by feeding death acceptance.

Then quantifiable faraway arms can be a conduit to really touch you.

2.

A clown disrupts complacency, so she needs him for aesthetic punishment.

Zany or awkward clown parts can be useful for thwacking her with crude thoughts, lust, greed, composite judgments.

Older outfits may feel remarkably tender, e.g., Monet, Arnold, Brueghel the Elder.

Use them in the name of sparkling lunacy, solar activism, wind trade, green blue wind flutter.

You might encounter urban wildlife floating down by you up river.

Read "you" as light entertainment, atomizing disposition, boat traffic, driftwood with knotholes, offshore fishermen.

After eight months of clown training, your everyday use value should be lustrously clever.

Try four clown honks to deflate regular economic bandwidths: what sneeze what snores what gray good cocks and
what treasures.

Why on pro bono, thee on pro bono.

Knot gardens are soul toys for seizing death acceptance.

3.

Fast moving clouds with gray underbellies momentarily block the visible light you have been impersonating.

Of course, you can't ever be that light so gratuitously warming up river molecules.

Let us now praise underlooked axiologies: blessed are the city's landfills, trash cans, graffiti wall murals.

What parts of her body share ancient parts with your body.

Multiply the results by those aforementioned 70 billion galaxies.

Assume sacrifice as a condition of value, then solve for clownwright.

Why thee on stalk is on stalk, as in between these fetters.

I direct "thee" at larger circulars, the way coupling in our homes ensures a beautiful utility.

As in chiastic intimate and cosmic space there should be little trouble situating the single person within the crosshairs of fragile galaxies.

Reader, in a clowned system, fools, silly transcendence become you.

4.

Sundown and waterdown regulate value in the perceiving subject, hypothetical cooperation of dominant and dominated, red, greenblue, violet wavelengths operating invisibly inside her.

Late sun is now imposing a yellow glareband on the river, every object in sight an ellipsis from the fish position.

Eighteen droplets may gather in the wind to impersonally kiss you.

She projects intricate knots, bends, hitches to prevent slippage in beloved values, forms of attention to equal thy attention: why on fastening, thee unfastening.

Receive, reader, intimate clownways to interlace you with gratuity, kindness, keeping you slightly ahead in a stream of something temporary, something expendable.

Then you can tie or untie knots in order of clown importance: Bhopal, river blindness, universal gun smuggling.

Generosity same as light, so perhaps you, thee, can perform a reckoning.

Unfortunately, global air pressure values will illuminate short range vehicles poised to gouge out aesthetic deceptions.

Even so, generosity could be dawn in you.

Like it or not, reader, in this venture, you and I have been coupling.

BLUE IN GREEN INTIMACY

I.

In your capacity as spirit in an afterlife, you'd have no limbs.

Here spirit is a remission word, so she can fasten a pot of his pink snapdragons to it.

The body contains spirit, moves it along.

Blue-gray branches of windlight break apart and come together all along the river, quick glimpse incarnations of at loose spirit ends.

Thick green trees on the nearby promontory are echoed in the river by muddy surface trees, displacing some of the blue-gray water stretches.

She sees the trees as form and not detail, afternoon preface to industrial buildings on the opposite shore becoming silhouettes at dusk, a little later.

The buildings will be backlighted by changing colors in the sky and foregrounded by the buildings' white and yellow shore lights, every night a stranger.

She hopes channeling expressions of less than holy river values won't be enough to disqualify quiet attempts at spirit making.

A particular spirit may be of use to one person and no use to another person, for example, Miles on horn, river glow.

Likewise my use of birds on the deck dispersing empty little seedhomes.

Her body needs spirit to need body *and* spirit, eke out motion, risk, birds of a feather, blue-green river flow.

Birds of a feather not always good at social-mirroring, turntaking.

Depending on circumstance, an individual spirit may be larger or smaller than the containing body, as in measure to measure your scale of response to lupus, Huntington's.

Biological limits on one measure sizing up another measure are conditioned by random variables, so her body is alternately an enabling and disabling mechanism.

2.

A light-adapted eye generally has its maximum sensitivity in the green region of the optical spectrum.

Did Miles know this; also that in some languages green and blue are not distinguishable.

Even so, an artist's primary colors are not the same as a poet's complementary colors defined by light mixtures.

The man and the woman encapsulate differences for depicting spirit in a containing body: water, wind, color temperature.

Sometimes he is blue light, sometimes he is green pigment, at other times, he switches between media.

My affect is shallow, because of medication for calming purposes, so in applying man body, woman body to a spirit canvas, "I give you what I can," under-emotionally.

Ordinarily his colors are cool colors in his relations with her but not cool in relation to his context with others' colors, flip-flopping associational temperatures, the way the hottest stars radiate blue light while red radiates from the coolest and you won't see this.

Yet warm blue colors in him come with her once each week regularly.

She lets him mistake warmth as sufficient for "being with," naming by negation the way she had long ago mistaken him.

Black, when added to a color, decreases mismatch on the man and the woman's compatibility scale.

It lets him take on hues captivating to a transitory female: blue, green, black, brushed by riverhome.

3.

Today I valued earwigs, dust mites, cultures with spirits who inhabited everything.

Miles did know this: modality.

Fortunately, the brain is not able to discriminate modalities with input from only one modal register.

Alone, "with" has no substance, but when joined by an object inflects a range of associative registers, as when a beloved comes to you with heart in mouth, with no holds barred, with the sun on.

She perceives spirit through this syntactical effect but names it eccentrically.

Spirit: membrane potential, thud, body tamer, inner radio.

Whether visible light is absorbed or reflected by nearby objects you see one another with those objects, as if handing spirit through instrument.

She sees him through tugs piloting the ships dropping off mounds of coal, rock salt.

The size of one's spirit shifts in the way windlight shifts perceptibly or imperceptibly, as with warming actions on mood, lice, chlorophyll, scattering a material person through scales of augmentation, diminishment.

Usually I am more blue than green because of uncertainty for when to start, when to stop with compassion, generosity toward who is this stranger.

Green: To stand your ground with; let down your guard with.

Blue: See another through disease, failure, petty behaviors, within a companionship.

Compare spirit to blue or green light you can't hold but can be held with.

Then hold her to blue in green spirit for enlarging the day, embouchure, horn, with Miles on mute intimacy.

PER SE INTIMACY

for Lee Teverow and Marjorie Milligan

I.

Imagine a soldier imagining you not imagining him.

Bracket any step he takes, buddy, witness, always being on, IED, clown porn, clowned geography.

The idea is to capture the worst stars, shove to the back of the mind homeland disengagement within a milky galaxy, sons, daughters, planetary marketing of children.

The clown relishes weeping irritants, herpes, poison ivy, useful for inducing hearty smearing manias.

Set clown value in relation to other intrinsic values, troop frustrations with higher up infighting: "wimps in Washington," General Stan McChrystal.

Witherdee, witherdee, her lingual artery.

At home, she toughs out Perseid meteor showers, August beach walking.

Underneath slow-burning galaxies the clown regulates intimate relations to the sacred via the jugular.

Spindle neurons generate her electrical clown feeling signals, flood her emotions with any night that's moonless, galactic clown rationing.

Marx himself would scarcely exclude from a work of art big red noses, transcendent humor.

Do you ask advice of your children.

Here's her squall line.

What the squall do you think when the liquid of a body cuts another body floating through it.

2.

Human emotions are rooted in the predictions of dopamine brain cells constantly readjusting their expectations in response to actual occurrences, effects of firefights, animal moisture.

Her moist line is connected to her head line, when the sea tumbles her.

Indignity is what makes her pratfalls diverting, modus ponens, dignity by means of indignity.

Figure too that at a beach a clown would moan in ecstasy from all that youth and sexual splendor.

What then is a good pick-me-up for taking on Kandahar's political temperature.

Her brain's feeling cells measure the mismatch between expectation and outcome when a little kid tries to help her.

All summer I have had no one to talk with about my behavior, all summer I have been pacing like a gull to see you.

Her dopamine neurotransmitters are the source of her emotional capacity for invisible analysis, tongue playing clown tag with the soldier.

Likewise, soldier wisecracking functions as a solidarity mechanism for neutralizing insurgent mathematics, homesickness, anybody feeling lethal, e.g., can't find his belly button, turtle fucking.

RC EAST: (ENEMY ACTION) DIRECT FIRE RPT (Small Arms) TF CHOSIN: 1 CIV KIA 2 CIV WIA

1645Z:D 26 REPORTS THAT THERE ARE 13–15 JINGLE TRUCKS ON FIRE AT THE ENTRANCE TO DAB VALLEY

True, soothing nonnumerical coordinates can be made available to relatives of a person given up, a person exchanged.

However, remote tribal areas, vast motivational incoherence will sorely test your ordinal integrity.

3.

Of the following, pick three balance points and become them, modifying the soldier.

A speckled bird lands on the railing of the deck, an inside girl asks, where is my mother.

Principles of harmony in air, water, salts give aesthetic order to density, hue, proportion, chastening clown want.

Sacrifice is a condition of value, also modifying the soldier.

The bereaved girl looks up, brain absorbing scary outerwear, randomness, moon magnifying rough laced cloud foam.

Off-balance you may consider homeostatic side effects stipulating clown betrayal.

Your want line connected to your fish line, your fish line connected to your moist line, your moist line connected to
    your _____.

She steps into herself.

The clown scatters her, before she can scatter him, waves rippling with her greed, carelessness, bigotry.

Per se clown silliness is no stranger to kinship with clown nastiness, both blowing off composure.

Let clausal misbehaviors signify synaptic callouts from this Afghanistan.

Swing low, sweet charity.

May the good clown bless you and keep you, soldier, victims of the soldier.

INSIDE OUT INTIMACY

I.

Over their bathing suits, departing beachgoers pull on their clothes

Public dressing an expertise that evolved, as did wisdom through cellular error

Barely concealed that wet or dry the red spot on the yellow gull beak throes alone

Mathematically call for duration, pitch in the contours of moist persons

The sea needs a body to mediate a body if, so like a window, all the great ones glow

To keep your head above water, seek will-unsettling actions, not action in already-settled wills

Memorial minute with one aunt and 37,373 Fenway Park strangers, like a wave, not naked, not form fitting

From here on out, in left breast stage one, caution, lest the littler suckers crack the nodes

Zany the etiologies beneath surf conditions and Carlyle's laughter

What are the limits in NASA's public images for immersing body and soul

Turn the fabric inside out before washing this garment

Agitated subaqueous molecules will tone down perception of the mouth's indivisibility

Reread *A Child's Garden of Verses*, Robert Louis Stevenson, yo ho ho

Make what was once close to your body close to my body

Find in floating a motive for time and space displacement, come or go

2.

What if dredging inside a personal history means taking out a child

More advantageous the inside-out flower's six reflexed petals pulling back from its stamens and pistil

Suppose it true Yörük tribe members chewed the leaves from *V. hexandra* as a medicine for their coughs

Does my submersion in a salt solution come out green and weaponly

First there now here, stones, pebbles rubbing one another back and forth

How like the genes a series of fault lines expresses synchronicity

A comparative grief here emulates indirect comprehension of the seabed

One intimacy two intimacy three intimacy four, nine griefs to the ocean surface, eleven griefs to the ocean floor

If I were a lighthouse keeper I'd have less company

Like Coleridge's demented mariner the clown brain moseys along

Deeply contradictory the mind's reactions to the body's unscrupulous data gathering

Over and over shadows from the circling flock sped ominously down the brick exterior of the old medical building

Picking parsley ahead of the frost, she accidentally brought into the kitchen tiny opportunistic flies

Like playing clown tag with the surf, what goods can you glean from weather watching

The surgeon knew where to cut into each breast by following screen shots of what was dividing inside

3.

Late one night a nursing home resident asks, what's deep in the heart of Texas

Six inches in Virginia, she upends me with the standard punch line

Why assume that at my clown expense an 80-something wouldn't enjoy a long and hearty laugh

Covering 71 percent of the earth's surface, oceans maintain an enormous privacy

I take pleasure in mnemonic spaces embedded in the five-lined staff

The Pentagon expresses shock shock at the release of its secret war logs

What is the difference between the gray then green line of my personal humbug

Sparkles in the water join the surf's reprise when replicating the sun with visual echoes

Whom to thank for building in me an obsessive recursiveness so much like the ocean's

I accept that as condition of the sentence inside words will be infiltrated by a surrounding blank

When he was younger, my father would carve names on the surface of growing pumpkins

At harvest the expanded names would be grownups in the finished scars

How irresistible other tumor-minded gourds bumped up as if bent on human fingering

When scientists find means to resurrect the body who will locate ones like me having no children

Before winter, take time to walk the sea as complement to the rolling dark

4.

Off my high horse accidently spilled on the green rug white dots made by my paper puncher

In his painting of the boats one of them seems to smile and have eyes

Wet down my meanness to set off molecular charges extending the interiors of these sentences

I juggle lines the way a juggler tosses objects, coordinating eyes and hands to perhaps intimate an inside out maneuver

Staring at length to catch the coarse-grained moment of each wave breaking, what matching molecular sequence made
     me so preoccupied

Stayed inside all day as if dropping the ocean

Or maybe dropped by the ocean all staid inside stayed inside

Do you prefer macro or micro modification as when a fluid lays you green in downed pastures

Believe me I've tried who or what being the center of our galaxies

On the scale of one to ten how much pain how much pain do you have

Before the entrance to the tunnel, the twilight beauty of the Boston skyline, windows gold, buildings all gray and silvery

Underwent airport scanning so the collective body would not be terrorized by the violable passages of my body

That inside job how greige and just, how unmanageable

On the scale of one to ten, mark where the breath shuns or panders to the blue or green smack of the ocean

Still leading me on the waters may be equal than but not lesser to what's companionable

5.

What local knowledge would make my flotsam and jetsam patterns visible

An itinerant clown might hold the line at let us pause not lettuce paws

How hard to hold the line with waterborne illnesses such as dysentery such as cholera

All together my efforts to whip up the ocean, like the ocean, would be no page-turners

Though they can project a briny respect for narrative on Melville on the movie *Jaws*

Who knows why I have set pens and pencils around the basin in my bathroom

Still difficult to talk about my body as if it were not my body

Not to mention that reconciling with a reconfigured body may take a while

Just as the stone's throw marks the limits to the integrity of my seafulness

In then out the moon breaks every night with its ancient style

Divide the ocean in half then cleave it then cleave it again

Pulled out from the parts more tide then less tide is still more tide

Riding a sequence may end with you tumbled out as if scraping the shoreline

Just as inside the channel markers there's a belling in the distance for what I tell what I will not tell

Intimacy a reverting of sound into silence but then this bell

GOOD NEIGHBOR INTIMACY

I.

Baseline imitation studies suggest mirror neurons may be beneficial for understanding another person's goals and intentions.

I see her move her hand, I move my hand.

I open my mouth and say "Ah" when she tells me to.

Guess what you are prone to, even if you don't consciously exhibit it.

Even in the normal brain a nerve cell may be unsweetly kissed by a variant.

Guess what just up star alley.

Guess what the emotive, the taxonomy of the emotive.

Merely witnessing an action makes mirror neurons fire in response to that action, so your brain simulates your neighbor's when you watch him throw out his recyclables.

An object's imminent graspability is encoded as an intimate aspect of the object's movement potential, his aluminum cans, fence posts, my crabapple.

Cutting up and removing fallen limbs may depend on empathetic mimicking of a tree's natural phase transitions.

The pinecone is falling, has fallen, is no longer a pinecone.

A circuit of multiple feedback loops enables the body's internal and external surveillance mechanisms.

Does she intend for her neighbor to catch her watching him.

On her property, deep blue hydrangeas, a purple butterfly bush abut with time and space, inject relief, commonality, within an infinite egress of witnessing.

2.

Fog drapes my neighborhood in the form of a seadragon.

The good neighbor trips, stumbles into the woodpile.

In the brain's map of the body, the map of the feet is next to the map of the genitals.

Between the legs, neighbor, ah, secrecy, arousal as you go along.

Guess what the curable, OK the incurable.

Scanty camouflage in an airy looking glass provokes water gossip in the mist, good neighbor telling or not telling on you.

Appealing to other values to justify a value is like describing musical redness to this person.

Even when her higher brain interprets the interplay of signals from various neural circuits and null blocks normally, a family of clowns keeps streaking through.

Each keeping structure may make patterned connections with other keeping structures, often forming healing circuits as diverse as emotional riches, telepathy, stride piano.

If proportionate keeping to yourself allows you to enjoy reciprocity with others while simultaneously preserving your individuality, what then accounts for Thomas Jefferson's abominable keeping behaviors at Monticello.

Guess what, fantasy, the brain's desire for fantasy.

Guess what, the clown as a choice between competitive shufflings.

Color perception is neurally linked to emotion, such as a blue or green sore spot within the neighbor.

My brain butterflies instead of settling.

3.

The mother would end lengthy conversations with "that's the story" and later the daughter would mirror this pattern.

Until then the daughter rarely spoke, except to neighboring starlight.

Rapid transmission of language, art, tools during the past 50,000 years has been attributed to an increase in the sophistication of the mirror neuron system.

Monogamous, nonmonogamous rays of light are all part of my neighborhood.

Say "ah" in anticipation of the red helleborine orchid mimicking the floral coloration of the bellflower in a bee's visual system, inducing the bee's pollination service.

You can see in the baby ducks floating on the pond animal pleasure.

Action and perception are intertwined in the brain, allowing the baby's sound patterns to be mapped onto the baby's motor patterns, quackety-quack quack, onomatopoeia.

One neighbor shoots another neighbor.

Survival of human tongue, palate, and lip muscles must have been beholden to a range of ancestral "no" inflections.

If Clown A steals five heads of lettuce from Clown B how long does it take B to seek revenge within the salad dressing.

The silent girl pretended Betelgeuse would be her husband, when she became a dead person.

She locked starry eyes with him.

An intimate keeping pattern could be identified by utilizing the nearest red neighbor algorithm.

Her make-believe might not follow logically, but it could follow beautifully, even when she was being pursued by star and tongue depressors.

4.

In neighboring brain regions, there is the star and the getting behind the words for the star, partner sounds broken up by incoming object reflections.

Even though "if" and "then" have no independent existence outside the neighborhood of the sentence, they cast a fine shadow.

Busybodies were mistaken if they thought the quiet girl would grow to have no mouth on her.

Guess what, one narrative faces off with another narrative.

Guess what, this little neuron went to market, this little neuron stayed here.

When I am not allowed to drive myself, my neighbor takes me to and from my round of medical procedures.

Mirror neurons, with their eye, ear, and motion sensors, can help with abstracting commonalities from other bodies, so maybe you can accommodate each neighbor becoming a different kind of neighbor, over the years.

Guess what a set of motion clowns figuring you in the mirror.

Guess what she spoke on condition of not telling me what I wanted to hear.

When I don't get what I want, body postures, eyes down, arms crossed, convey my ugly red mood and intentions, like Lucy mirroring Harpo.

Mirror representation extends beyond the scope of good will mimicry, one clown beating on another clown, landscape with moon and a mockingbird.

Let tonight be the night we go circle dancing.

In ritual steps let us lighten up to the effects of being differentials.

Until then, good neighbor, come in, I'll hold the door but wipe your feet before entering.

SO DISPOSED INTIMACY

after G. C. Waldrep

The wave's existence does not depend on its being experienced by a conscious subject. The seaweed's existence does not depend on its being experienced by a conscious subject. Blue whale breath seeks ant mortician does depend on voluminous experiences with a conscious subject. When the harbor clown seals up, the seals seal up. Is this perseveration, is this a holding.

For many days I wondered about my water retention. Blue whale breath greets ant mortician. Mindful awareness of the sea to which you are holding requires a left and right hemisphere, requires a coping. This one is sweeping and that one is leaping. If you get my drift is there an intimacy, is there a bend in the cooperative eye to see if an other is unfolding. This is an elision. This is an evening. This is a floating.

Match a red herring with three other red herrings to swim to the next level, let's call it "component parts of ocean." Are you suspicious of flowerlike animals, are you suspicious of the rock-clinging scarlet psolus. In the cooperative eye there is this arabesque, there is this neural mission for species lumping. Blue whale breath freaks ant mortician. Can you name ten taxonomic categories that could benefit from "move it along" transpositions. Is there a need to mention the returning soldier.

Put your fingers here. Is this the right spot. No here, put them here. Where does the comb jelly come from, what are its digestive patterns, how far in its comings and goings. We interrupt this interruption for the sake of groping. Let's not get carried away with the more or less tractable sea inhabitants, the water's being or not being fungible. Blue whale breath breeds further ant morticians. Here we go barging in. How could you not detect a pattern of clowns inside the book of numbers.

What is touch. A touch can be a suspect, can be a blowhole, can be a snuggling. Blue whale death yields to ant morticians. If even a tube worm can be expressed as a numeric function, what is war, war is an undeciding factor, in war there is an enumerated body outnumbered by a cast of mechanisms. So might you insert an electronic chip to transfer mindfulness to the ensuing bacteria. Will the culprit be in this one or that one. Can you reinstall to one more intimate promise. In this the culprit. I doubt it. No.

ON YOUR MARK INTIMACY

Two and two are slate. Two and three are lime. Here is the oldest gesture. Here is the oldest dime. My left leg was sucked into a sinkhole. Here is a word I like: plastered. Here is another word I like: quire. Here is where I was a dimwit about apparitions. Here the sea nearly took back my hide.

How many clowns does it take to titillate a light bulb. There is the air-raid clown, there is the anchor clown, there is the clown who has hair. I suspect I like the wrong kinds of light bulbs. How many to charge up meaningful sentences. How many to keep apart old moon from new moon, how many climbings with flair.

Now we'll talk about Victor Borge. Now we'll talk about Cher. One locomotion doesn't represent another locomotion. One stair doesn't represent another stair. The Puritans were champions at text messaging. They locomoted to a universe of signs. Dear present day generations: You'll have twenty seconds to outperform the Puritans on WTF radio. Try not to miss the mark in the staging area. Try not to commence second guessing at the starting line.

Is the race between the US and the metric system. Is the race between narrow and wide. Contestants should have read the Psalms and Ecclesiastes. Contestants should have biked through at least New Mexico and Arizona. Contestants should want to pay tithes. Will the reality principle knock over intimacy protection barriers. Will there be a need to go beyond music and wine.

Each race demands a certain type of audience. This one is a race about visual processing. This one is a race about crime. Here is a race about shifts in tonality. Here are races with variable finish lines. Each race scattershots a primary leg of difficulty. Each race compromises the audience's equilibrium. Each racer competes in more than one race at one time.

LUNGE INTIMACY

Like a river drawn down to clown pathographies:
what one cannot smell out one may smell into:

As if in another: world: as if in your own world's: value space: there: might like: recasting that pig: its lungs its snout: spread cahoots with: breaking: laws of scale: post: clown force winds: post: down on farm alley: energy but indifferent energy: you hoot you hinge: wild nurse to: manured old soul: might like: clown lip clown doxology: relationship status: goats: to wall in wall out: not the first: not the last: to go down with: phantom body: let horseflies: lunge under: lunge over: it

Whatever: viral musters is viral touched: whence: solitude: whence: communication: hash sentiment: hash olfactory: with burred left leg: go nosey on down: past: last raw ledge: past: last raw hill: until: to bind: retrace: bootscent: odor receptor: wild pear: milkweed: thistle: befriend malva: befriend mud: for when you: fields to river: lunge fête: lunge asymptote: lunge alternate ways of crabappling it:

But when at bottom: helper clowns: pop up: clutch: as at: your river face your: river throat: how to: brakescent: clown divisions: clown accrualbooks: from whence this world's: cowpaths thickets allergens: stink: expand: stir up with: whole farm dues: at which: beyond: your indwelling out your: indwelling in: lunge: clown purposes: clown indexicals:

LAWS OF MOTION INTIMACY

after Anja Utler

1.

Leg asleep: shake out: how far it to: etch: calibrate
line stave: line industry
then shoo then gasp
whose: overbearing: who'd:
here mordants here fiddleheads: you etch you calibrate: there woundtights: there: tree
    scavengers: how come: you spool you thread: you go come too: as when: where
    underneath: you would what comes: you would what goes: and now: linecocked:
    now enterturned: what if: in so
short a romp: you tramp: skip: leg along: for: in if: would's amplitude: here's touched:
    now go:

Then horns: unhinged: miles: stake out: vinecracked:
full: throttle: full throttle through: windsoaked: throat: glottis:
horn away: as with the skullcaps: marshed: stalked: and shear-
cropped blue: blow on: and air-exceed the limits of: as when: mad-dogged: besotted:
    skewed:
I let clowned fields set heels-a-light set heels-a-lieu: spoked: blare-
fed: which would you through; and then: why-installed: you: addleculled: addlesowed:
    for then: once
there: and leaning-to: what then from hence: from addled hew: to whet: how come the
    mindthrusts herded oversong: how come: in wouldstock: added rue: added
    woodranks: added rue

2.

Of course: I fell: root-tripped then splat: clown at bottom: with
tadpoles laughed enough to scare the daylights out: if line off-track *is* line on-track: at
    whom went wild: went aiming at: then

almost: how come: almost went black:
instead: as if in sun-net: song kept on: and reached the bank:
for: how much: how far: would mind made up of
line ablame: untimed: unbuttoned: cracked: care
less: for whom: at bottom: celldecides: then seeps up: through: unawareness level second
        first: above whose value spliced

and spliced: breeds miles: for whence: how come: cellconstrained: nests: thickets: reeds:
        so undesigned: co-
here: enough to-get-her: worried wild: for so conjoined with that:
and in that mood went on: so addlehewed: so addlewed: until:: marshstopped::
I watched nighthawks learn to clown contend:
though not enough to quiet: marsh unrest: from where
at bottom: line: re-goes the urge: to re-dis-tribute: cell: re-dis-tribute: hike: as though
you would redo: line's turn: to horn away and air-exceed the limits of: clown made your
        bed: clown lies in it

FALL TO FALL INTIMACY

wah-wah: clown went a-sportin' ah she did go

well: uh huh

ONCE UPON A TIME INTIMACY

Forgive us this day my slew

of

clown compulsions

RESUMPTION INTIMACY

I.

A sandpiper flits ahead of her along the shore until a gull
swoops and scares it away, recasting bird boundaries,
air sea earth patterns a walker
steps into, voluntary associations with colorful
seashore implements, sand sculptures. Underfoot
the high tide closing in motions up her memorybird impulses.
She has a seabrained disposition—small sand dollar, white stone,
orange stone, three larger stones with black, green, orange flecks
in hand. See in me as you wish, my night nest name, the dead
resuming in a bird, metempsychosis,
mother to daughter to daughter
passages, day handy in footprints, bird over human, human
on top of bird, wet sand, dry sand, particles, waves ratcheting up
for impending low tide convergences.
Some think blank slate models ideal for entertaining
"not me" practices, but she thinks damaging information,
sea swipe, salt scrub, perpetual in and out ID rituals.
What of the convicted killer in her family on her paternal side,
no one she knows, but of course people can google it.
She was trailing the bird as an intimate walk companion,
exclusive, like a good in itself, sound shapes willed, unwilled,
sex, affection, housework, health care, advice, conversation,
companionship. Really, she was stalking the bird, just as in dreams
she dreams her bird sicknesses. Trust and risk are involved,
the body of the mother in the sandpiper asking for it.

2.

The landing gull may have been white with a gray back.
Whenever a bird comes near she startles before the bird,
as if mother, daughter had summoned one another's hidden
personhoods. Who goes there.
A bird is then twinned, a private public object
you can't isolate from the predatory biological world
where it might become a value-will issue, mixing allowances,
pecking orders, remittances. No household lasts long
without extensive economic interaction among its bird members.
And what is the media used to represent bird value in these bird
systems. Fees, bribes, tips, donations of eggs, blood, organs
come up regularly, noticeable in genetic transmission
boundaries, time-outs undercutting sin sentiment,
any stones in hand, vindication, birth children:
surely by now you have googled my name
seeking out the criminal's. Whither
shall I watch for you. She is tied like that to the bird,
the way water brings out color in beach stones,
choice management, instrumentality, undercover
stoning impulses. Or is she preying on you
in the form of a bird, distributing and consuming your goods
as hers, extending ties across boundaries into other settings,
pairing swimmer, water rat, lifeguard, turkey vulture.
How old are your dreams. Who are you in that far from land
petrel: Wind-blasted. Sea-skimming. Whither
shall I watch for you. "You" not easily containable
when pulled together inside a bird.

3.

Lying awake in the dead of night she wonders
which is the bird that first starts all the others' AM singing.
I am going to market for possessed glass, buying me
a pitcher to hold schools, armies, churches, sometimes
their termination. Can you damage a bird's social standing
when all these flocking relations generate
their own forms of wacky transfers and trust is asymmetrical.
How old are your dreams. One morning in a steamed-up mirror,
thick white circles around widening brown eyes no nose
barely a mouth: gray waterlogged face, goggle/halo eyes
in owl head, a monster daughter image.
Flash back to memory acquisition, pulse, shared secrets,
interspecies meanings: rules, body information, body services,
resumption rituals. Look, under terms of endearment, a precarious
co-habiting: trash, shame, sloppy habits, tedium. Away
from voyeuristic third parties, one first bird does too
start all the others singing.
In spheres you seek to expand and contract, everyday graphics,
my daughter hand where you rubbed it, no black or blue
bruisings, fewer age spots, on which intimacy could prosper.
Is this a more authentic feathering. What am I supposed
to. Lower your voice. Calm down
to a feigning focus no more than necessary.
Bird in the mouth, mouth in the bird: scavenger, token,
parent, visitor: yes no: integral choice more choice than in mirror-
looking: who are you anyway: question to mark, mark as to bird:
how old in your dreams, your halo-eyed flights, birds, beach
stones, whither will I watch for you, your out and out
shift-shapes, your sandpiper my owl head pulling together
light tides dark tides, as in any bird, any human.

WING INTIMACY

for Bradford Robinson

There is a pier extending into the channel and docks with shacks along the boardwalk.

We pick one shack we sit in front of it.

This is just a value sketch for bestowing fishing-village objects, out-of-wind fortitude, winter watercolor.

One person sits on the ladder/ramp to the door of the shack.

The other sits on a plastic gasoline carrier near the dock's pilings.

The ladder/ramp has strips of wood nailed onto it for foot gripping.

Rope, barrels, chains, lobster pots, spars, hoses, anchors, wire, gaff, pails: seasonal workspace absent strangers
      bequeath to occupying strangers: bright day lit up, as on the bias; emotional coding, there, without intending.

Come touch to come go, local value space to wind value space, dispersal narratives bracketed from refurbishing
      technique, caress, graze, caress, solid dock over ephemeral dock, blue-green water color under brushstroke,
      brushstroke over empathy.

You can hear availability error in the bells, gulls, the rubbing of the boats against their fenders.

Some of the shacks along the dock have broken windows.

It has been a mild December so far, many days in the 50s.

Two scoop nets on the far side of the shack we have inherited.

All the sides of this one are simply sheets of board, not shingles.

Fish tails and fins also, nailed to the anterior of the shack we are in front of.

Some of the fins look like wings, but he says no no, they are just fins, probably.

You can see dried blood, oily black film, ragged flesh where the tails and fins were hacked by the fisherman.

Imagine: A me first: off with their heads. A me next: off with their bodies. A me after: post hoc justification, a series of boastings.

Real wings, these have to be wings, on the other side of the shack, not visible to him.

Shall I title my sketch "Menemsha: Bird, Anger at" or "Sample Americana: Empathy."

You can count the shafts of the feathers, but they are disintegrating feathers, some already missing, others becoming matted. Start over.

Bird wings, fish tails, fins, display of: me leaning on the shack wall, counting body parts and then sunning.

I was there but can't mount for you a motor-valued summary.

My wildlife anatomy: bookish; my vision memory: sketchy.

The channel markers bend hard against the incoming tide: red right return: see, that I remember.

I who am nearly always jumping out of my skin: serenity.

We were there, he planned it, one more time, together at this place, unexpectedly.

All of us into us: fishing industry: boats, dock, shack, tools: red point of red return: value stretch caught in neural machinery: moral grammar into throat halyard, mouth gag: prefrontal cortex times amygdala, fight or flight fidelity.

The tide is strong, it pulls the brown gray cormorants swimming up the channel backwards.

He is at the edge of the dock, quiet, looking at the opposite side of the channel, the boats and the hill cottages, not quiet, full of motion, in his sketching.

Now hear this: somatic internal organization a function of fixation, intimacy like height of fashion, laughter, endurance, plausibility; retaliation scale raising or lowering actor-observer bias; recency effect: one person's outrage another's idyll.

The sun, I am standing in the sun, probably red-faced, sea-coated.

The day is cold but not bone-chilling.

At Menemsha, relative worth to hue, saturation, lightness; revenge trophy as breath of fresh air under a troubled wingspan: air enough to come touch the go of it.

NOTES

"Larghetto Intimacy": Approximately one quarter of the language on selective mutism has been taken, some verbatim, some with varying degrees of modification, from "The Quiet Child: A Literature Review of Selective Mutism," by Sally Standart and Ann Le Couteur in *Child and Adolescent Mental Health* 8.4: 2003. "Inhumanity of the linguistic code" is from Mutlu Blasing's *Lyric Poetry: The Pain and the Pleasure of Words*. "Nonaccountable spectatorship" reworks a phrase from Eve Kosofsky Sedgwick's *Epistemology of the Closet*.

"Thing Intimacy": A few words and phrases have been borrowed from Bill Brown's essay "Thing Theory" in *Critical Inquiry* 28.1: 2001.

"Laws of Motion Intimacy": Some phrases have been borrowed and reworked from Mutlu Blasing's *Lyric Poetry*, Henry Fountain's "Hiking around in Circles? Probably, Study Says" (*New York Times* 8.21.09) and *Going Afoot*, by Bayard Christy (1920). Military slang is from the "Unofficial Unabridged Dictionary for Marines" compiled by Glenn B. Knight.

"On Your Side Intimacy": A few phrases have been borrowed from Daniel Kahneman's *Thinking, Fast and Slow*, some verbatim, some nearly verbatim. "Loose spirit" is from Annie Dillard's *For the Time Being*.

"Do No Harm Intimacy": Some phrases have been borrowed and reworked from Mark Greif's essay "Cavell as Educator," *n+1*, *#12*; Sam Harris's *The Moral Landscape: How Science Can Determine Human Values*; Brian Christian's *The Most Human Human: What Artificial Intelligence Teaches Us About Being Alive*; Jennifer Kahn's "Can You Call a 9-Year-Old a Psychopath?" *New York Times Magazine* 5.13.12; the *Downton Abbey* TV series; and Kathryn Schulz's *Being Wrong: Adventures in the Margin of Error*. The line "unlike earlier thinkers" in section 3 is quoted verbatim from *Being Wrong*.

Château Noir is the name of a painting by Paul Cézanne. Mrof reverses the word "form."

"Free Will Intimacy": Sources for some of the language include: Viviana A. Zelizer, *The Purchase of Intimacy*; Robert Kane, *A Contemporary Introduction to Free Will*.

"To the Letter Intimacy": "Intimacy bears this moral charge" reworks a phrase from Viviana A. Zelizer's *The Purchase of Intimacy*. "Emotional division" has been borrowed from Eva Illouz's *Cold Intimacies: The Making of Emotional Capitalism*. Bubble information is reworked from material taken from Wikipedia.

"Street Intimacy": Some terminology has been borrowed from James Trefil's *A Scientist in the City*, and from Calvin Morrill and Edward Snow: "The Study of Personal Relationships in Public Places" in *Together Alone: Personal Relationships in Public Places*. The theater referred to is the Lederer Theater, formerly known as the Majestic Theater, in Providence, Rhode Island.

"To the Reader Intimacy": A few phrases have been borrowed and reworked from John Guillory's chapter "The Discourse of Value" in his *Cultural Capital: The Problem of Literary Canon Formation*. "What sneeze . . . what treasures" clowns around with the first line of Eliot's "Marina."

"Blue in Green Intimacy": "Blue in Green" is the title of the third track from Miles Davis's album *Kind of Blue*. "Even so . . . light mixtures" is reworked from a sentence on color theory from Wikipedia. "A light-adapted eye . . . optical spectrum" is nearly verbatim from an August 2010 article on the visible spectrum from Wikipedia.

"Per Se Intimacy": Some of the language has been borrowed and reworked from John Guillory's chapter "The Discourse of Value" in *Cultural Capital*, Michael Hastings's *Rolling Stone* article "The Runaway General," Jonah Lehrer's *How We Decide*, and Michael Bala's essay "The Clown: An Archetypal Self-Journey." The lines in all caps were taken from a us military war log posted on WikiLeaks in July 2010.

"Good Neighbor Intimacy": Some phrases and sentences have been borrowed, some verbatim, some nearly verbatim, from V. S. Ramachandran's *The Tell-Tale Brain: A Neuroscientist's Quest for What Makes Us Human* and L. Anders Nilsson's article "Mimesis of Bellflower (*Campanula*) by the Red Helleborine Orchid *Cephalanthera Rubra*."

"So Disposed Intimacy": Some words and phrases have been borrowed from V. S. Ramachandran's *The Tell-Tale Brain* and Brian Christian's *The Most Human Human*.

"Lunge Intimacy": "What one cannot smell out one may smell into" reworks a line spoken by the Fool in *King Lear*.

"Resumption Intimacy": Some of the language (with varying degrees of modification) has been borrowed from Viviana A. Zelizer's *The Purchase of Intimacy*.

ACKNOWLEDGEMENTS

Grateful acknowledgement is made to the editors of the following publications where versions of these poems first appeared:

Aufgabe: "Thing Intimacy," "Laws of Motion Intimacy" ("I watched an inchworm")
Brown Literary Review: "Per Se Intimacy"
Conjunctions: "Larghetto Intimacy," "Resumption Intimacy," "Wing Intimacy"
New American Writing: "To the Reader Intimacy," "Blue in Green Intimacy"
Petri Press: "Lunge Intimacy," "So Disposed Intimacy," "Whom Do You Trust Intimacy"
Tarpaulin Sky: "Free Will Intimacy," "Hinge Intimacy"
Web Conjunctions: "Rush Intimacy" (under the title "Rush"), "Château Noir Intimacy,"
　　　"To the Letter Intimacy," "Loop the Loop Intimacy," "Laws of Motion Intimacy"
　　　("Leg asleep")

The author wishes to thank the Rhode Island State Council on the Arts for a 2011 fellowship grant in poetry.

Special thanks to Lee Teverow and Marjorie Milligan for reading versions of this manuscript. Much gratitude to Michael Harper, who set me on this road many years ago. And as always, deepest love and appreciation to Reginald Shepherd, who is sorely missed.

This book was set in Candara and Centaur MT
by the Center for Literary Publishing
at Colorado State University.
Copyedited by Kaelyn Riley.
Proofread by Kristin George Bagdanov.
Interior designed & typeset by Ben Findlay.
Cover designed by Stephanie G'Schwind.